Emily,
Angel of the Yukon

Emily, Angel of the Yukon
Copyright © 2021 by Mary de Chesnay

All rights reserved. No part of this publication may be reproduced, distributed, or transmitted in any form or by any means, including photocopying, recording, or other electronic or mechanical methods, without the prior written permission of the author, except in the case of brief quotations embodied in critical reviews and certain other non-commercial uses permitted by copyright law.

Tellwell Talent
www.tellwell.ca

ISBN
978-0-2288-5940-6 (Hardcover)
978-0-2288-5939-0 (Paperback)
978-0-2288-6809-5 (eBook)

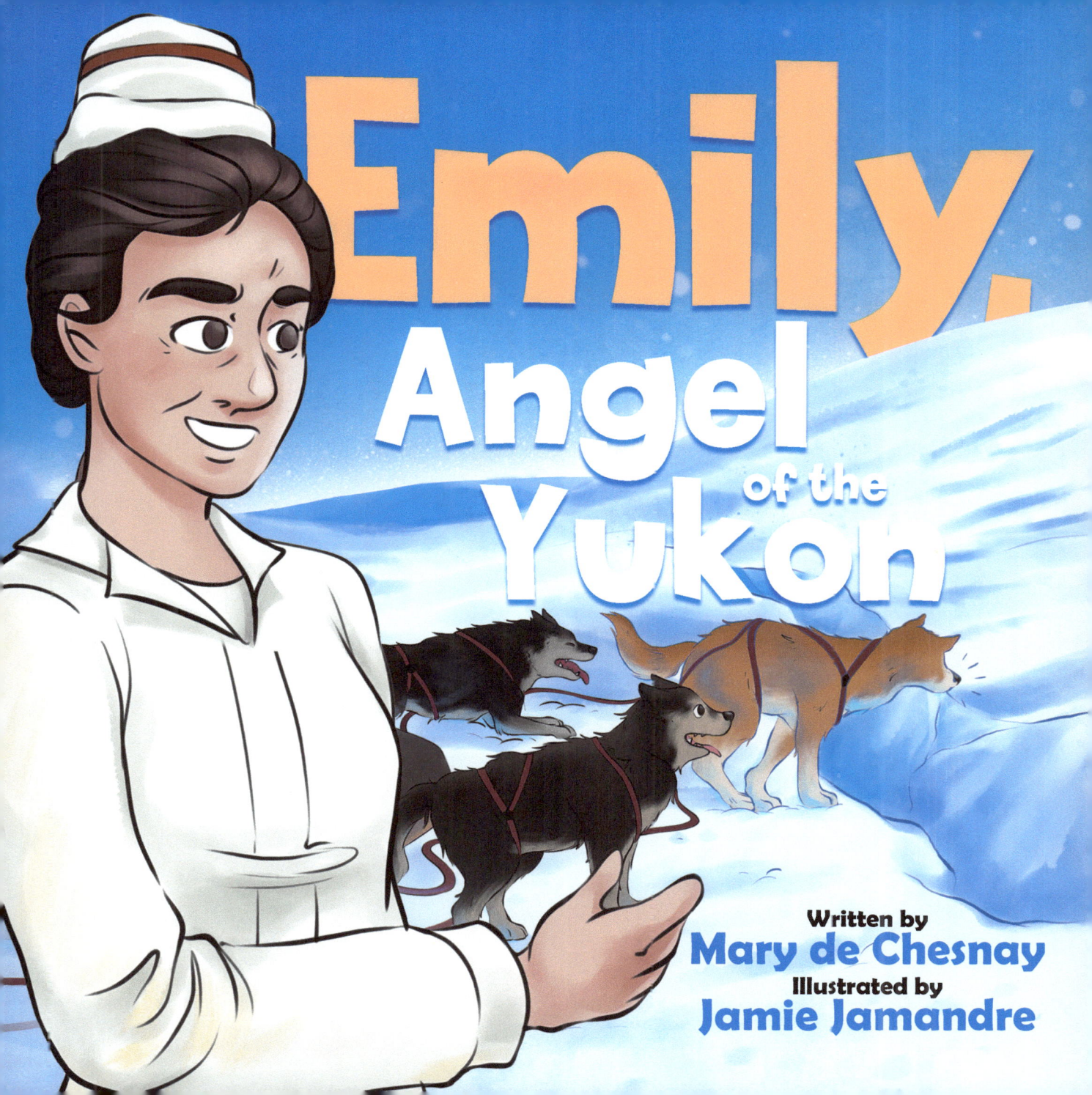

Dedication

For Heather Hughes Lewis from your recently discovered godmother MdC

Acknowledgments

The author is grateful to Grace Morgan Eckel and Kristine Eckel Rauenzahn for their memoir of Grace's sister, Emily Morgan, Angel of the Yukon, which includes Emily's personal account of her life in Alaska. I appreciate the encouragement of one of my oldest friends, Terri Appelhaus, to go ahead with this project. This book was published by the amazing team at Tellwell including Mary Apple Bertulfo, who answered about a hundred questions; Grace Gange, my project manager who oversaw the production from start to finish; Jen MacBride, my wonderful editor who helped me write better; Illustrator Jamie Jamadre, Designer Krystal Eve Roque and Ralph Cavero.

Table of Contents

Chapter One: *Quarantine*
Chapter Two: *Race Across the Snow*
Chapter Three: *Saving Lives*
Chapter Four: *Back to Normal*

Foreword

The story of the great dog sled race across Alaska to deliver diphtheria antitoxin to Nome, Alaska in 1925 has been told through the voices of the mushers, scholars, and journalists who justifiably highlight the ordeal of the mushers and the heroics of the dogs. Togo went the farthest, and Balto entered Nome on the last leg of the journey with the serum. The Iditarod Race, which was started to honor the tradition of dog sledding, commemorates the Great Serum Run that saved so many lives. This book tells what happened before and after the race. Emily Morgan was the designated diphtheria nurse who administered the serum to the Native Alaskans – mostly Inuit and some Yupik who were then called Eskimos. (The term Eskimo is no longer considered correct by Indigenous people because it was a name imposed on them by the white settlers. Emily would have used the term Eskimo, but here we use Inuit and Yupik for accuracy.) Emily trudged on foot through blizzard conditions with her medical bag to deliver the life-saving drug. Newspaper accounts at the time recognized her with the name, Angel of the Yukon. After her death, she was honored by being appointed to the Alaska Women's Hall of Fame. Emily Morgan, March 7, 1878 – May 8, 1960.

Chapter One
Quarantine

Nurse Emily Morgan trudged through the deep snow to the hut of an Inuit family whose little girl Anna was sick. She removed the thermometer from the child's armpit and frowned as she looked at the high reading. The little girl's tonsils were covered with a dark membrane. Emily recognized the disease as diphtheria. Emily remembered having this disease as a young woman, and she knew what it could do to people. She remembered being weak and unable to breathe. Fortunately, Emily received the antitoxin and recovered. Now, looking at little Anna, Emily had a bad feeling.

When Emily visited another Inuit family, she saw another very sick little girl who was so weak she could not open her mouth to be examined. Later, Emily went back to check on her, but her little brother said she had gone to heaven. The heartbroken father was making a casket for his daughter. Because of the quarantine, no one could come to bring him a casket. Emily removed her heavy gloves and coat and helped him. He tenderly laid little Mary in the casket with her clothes and toys. The ground was too frozen to bury her, so he put her on his dog sled and took her to a snowbank until spring.

Meanwhile, at the hospital, Dr. Welch saw a little boy named Billy. Dr. Welch thought Billy had tonsillitis. Billy went home. Sadly, he died the next day.

When Emily returned to the hospital, she told Dr. Welch about the children she had visited in their homes.

"Dr. Welch, I know you thought Billy had tonsillitis, but I'm afraid it was diphtheria. That means many more people are going to get sick. They could die."

Dr. Welch and Emily knew they did not have enough antitoxin for an epidemic.

An epidemic means that many people could get very sick and some could die. Diphtheria is a disease that is passed from person to person through the air. Antitoxin is a drug that kills the germ that causes the disease.

Dr. Welch had some old antitoxin but he was afraid it would not work. Medicines are only good for a while. Like food, medicines can spoil and even be dangerous.

It was January, and Nome was iced in. The last ship had already left Nome. No ships could enter the icy harbor. No airplanes could land. There were no roads for cars. The town was isolated. People were scared.

The town leaders called an emergency meeting. Dr. Welch told the leaders,

"You must quarantine people in their homes. Diphtheria is a bad disease that transmits easily from person to person. People cannot breathe and they die. Two children have died and more families are sick. The antitoxin I have is old and not safe to use. We must quarantine and bring fresh serum to Nome right away!"

The leaders knew the ships could not dock and the planes could not land. They started to panic, until one man said:

"The dogs will save us! There is serum in Anchorage. Send it north by train to where the train ends, and then set up dog sled relays across the ice to Nome. We can ask our best mushers to bring the serum to Nome."

And so they did. Emily was appointed the Diphtheria Nurse because she was the only nurse who had experience caring for people in their homes. During an epidemic it is important to keep people from spreading the disease to each other, so the sick people of Nome were quarantined in their homes. They could not be treated in the hospital.

Emily visited a Yupik home where a little girl named Vivian was so scared that she refused to open her mouth. Emily talked quietly with her. Suddenly, she asked to pray. The mother and child prayed in their language and then they recited the Lord's Prayer in English with Emily. The child said "Quyana" which means "Thank you" in Yupik. She then allowed Emily to examine her. Sure enough, Emily could see the dark membrane on her tonsils. Vivian had diphtheria. Emily gave some of the old serum to the child. She went back the next day and saw that Vivian had improved. Emily said a prayer of thanks that the old medicine had worked. This child would live!

Chapter Two
Race Across the Snow

Twenty mushers and 150 dogs started the run in the southeastern part of Alaska. The mushers were men who lived in the far north. The mushers carried people and supplies to remote places because there were no roads in those days.

The dogs were mostly Siberian Huskies with thick fur coats and beautiful blue eyes. Mushers came from all over Alaska and assigned themselves to stations along the way so they could relay the serum all the way across Alaska. To reach Nome, they would have to travel almost 700 miles far to the northwest. They picked up the serum from the train and bundled it in furs to keep it from freezing. Then, they set out on their lifesaving race to save the people of Nome. Winter was harsh.

The winds whipped the dogs and the mushers. Blizzards were common. Some dogs did not make it, yet the mushers hurried on with the precious serum. Some of the teams were stronger than others, and some were not able to go far.

The team that traveled the longest distance was led by a musher named Sepp and his Siberian Husky named Togo. Togo was getting old but he was smart. He was a natural leader of his pack. Sepp knew Togo would do his job! When Sepp packed up the serum, he said to Togo:

"OK, boy, this is the race of our life and we are going to win it!"

Togo understood. With a shake of his husky body and a wag of his tail, he seemed to say,

"I'm ready – let's go."

Togo led Sepp and the other dogs on a trail only he could sense. He led them over frozen water. One time the ice cracked and they almost fell into the frigid sea, but Togo stopped just in time for them to back away. He led them up and down steep ravines. A dog fell and almost plunged them all into a place where they would be stuck. But Togo stopped so Sepp could pick up the fallen dog.

There were way stations where Sepp and dogs could rest and eat some dried fish. Sepp rubbed wax on the pads of the dogs' paws to keep the ice from cutting their feet. Sepp did not rest long. He knew how important this trip was to the people of Nome. They were counting on him. Sepp was counting on Togo.

Chapter Three
Saving Lives

Finally, the serum was handed off to the last team, and a man named Gunnar and his dog Balto entered Nome in the dark early hours of the morning. When they arrived at the hospital, Emily was amazed to see them. The teams had made the trip in only five and a half days when everyone had expected it would take 15 days!

Now Emily had to deliver the serum to the people. Emily was ready! She wore several layers of leggings, a wool dress, and a sweater. Over her thick socks, she pulled on heavy fur boots called mukluks. She carried only a small medical bag with the serum, tongue depressors, a thermometer, and candy for the children. The winds were fierce and it was snowing so much she could barely see. Icy pellets stung her eyes and her face felt frozen. Yet she walked miles to reach all the homes of people in quarantine.

At one house, an Inuit mother and her baby were both sick. Emily had only two doses of serum left that night. She offered to give one dose to both the baby and the mother, but the mother said:

"No, give one to my son, but save the other in case another child is sick."

Emily was grateful to this generous woman because that night she found another child who needed the serum. Fortunately, Emily was able to return to the mother the next day to give her the serum. The mother recovered.

Chapter Four
Back to Normal

When the serum had been given to the people, and they were no longer sick, a giant sense of relief lifted the spirits of the villagers and townspeople. Quarantine ended. Men could open their businesses. People in town could once again gather in church to pray together. They opened their social clubs to dance and listen to music. Inuit fathers could resume hunting and fishing. Inuit mothers sewed furs again to make clothing for their family. Children played happily in their homes and in the snow.

Emily, too, could rest and do fun things. She and a friend took a long dog sled trip to Hot Springs, Alaska, where Emily took a bath outdoors in a small pool. The water was so hot she had to cool it down with ice! It felt so good to be clean after the long trip.

After the epidemic was over, Emily had her first airplane ride! A pilot had crashed and was stranded on a glacier for several weeks without food or shelter. He was so weak, but he badly wanted to go home to Anchorage to his wife and children. The doctor said he could go if Emily went along to care for him. She was thrilled to look out the window and see the glittering snow and ice and the trails of the dog sleds far below. Emily gave the pilot food and water and made sure he rested. He wanted to fly the plane. After all, he was a pilot, but Emily reminded him how much he needed to rest so that he could play with his children. His family was so happy to see him and he thanked Emily for taking such good care of him

"You are truly an angel, Miss Morgan!"

Another time, Emily and a friend skied to another friend's house to visit and have dinner. The house was buried in the snow and they could just barely get inside. Suddenly, they heard a clatter on the roof! It couldn't be Santa Claus – it wasn't Christmas Eve. Two of their friends had skied onto the roof, thinking it was just a snowbank!

The serum run was so famous that many newspapers sent reporters to tell the world about the heroic dogs and the nurse and the doctor who saved the people. The news reporters called Emily the Angel of the Yukon! Emily was so loved by the people of Alaska that they made her an honorary Pioneer. This honor was normally only given to people who had lived for many years in Alaska. Emily had only been there a few years. But the people knew that without her nursing skill and courage in administering the serum out in the villages, many more of them would have died.

Emily lived to serve as a nurse in WWII with the Red Cross. She finally retired to her home in Kansas, but she always said:

"Living in Alaska was the highlight of my life."

Glossary

Inuit and Yupik – Native (Indigenous) Alaskans who used to be called Eskimo.

Diphtheria – a disease that makes it hard to breathe. People can die of diphtheria, but there is an antitoxin or serum that can be given to stop the disease. Today, babies receive a vaccine against diphtheria and two other diseases called whooping cough and tetanus. Children and adults receive booster shots. Because we have a vaccine, those three diseases are rare and easily controlled.

Glacier – a huge mass of ice and rocks that slowly moves along in the coldest lands and seas.

Quarantine – a rule that says people must stay in their homes when a disease breaks out so that more people do not catch the disease. Quarantine is not necessary for all diseases, just for ones that are easily passed through the air or by touch.

Musher – a person who drives the dog sled. The musher cares for his dogs at home, and then he hitches them up to a sled to carry supplies and people to places in the snowy north where cars cannot go. When Emily lived in Alaska, mushers were men. Today, many women are mushers.

Serum – another name for antitoxin, serum is a drug made to reverse the effects of a toxic disease.

Iditarod Race – every February, teams of dogs and mushers in Alaska honor the history of dog sledding by racing from Anchorage to Nome in memory of the great serum run of 1925.

Bibliography

Eckel, G. M. (2017). *Angel of the Yukon*. Newton, Kansas: Mennonite Press.

Salisbury, G., & Salisbury, L. (2003). *The cruelest miles*. New York, NY: W.W. Norton.

About the Author

Mary de Chesnay, PhD, RN, PMH-BC, FAAN, is a nurse-anthropologist, teacher, and researcher who wants children to be as excited about reading as she is. Retired now, she makes jewelry under the supervision of Travis, the Airedale, and Tina Turner, the Shih Tzu, to raise money for animal rescues. She has written 16 books for nurses and researchers. Mary donates the proceeds of her writing to organizations that support vulnerable people and animals.

www.ingramcontent.com/pod-product-compliance
Lightning Source LLC
LaVergne TN
LVHW071651060526
838200LV00029B/427